ANIMAL SKIN & SCALES

David M. Schwartz *is an award-winning author of children's books, on a wide variety of topics, loved by children around the world.* Dwight Kuhn's *scientific expertise and artful eye work together with the camera to capture the awesome wonder of the natural world.*

For a free color catalog describing Gareth Stevens Publishing's list of high-quality books and multimedia programs, call 1-800-542-2595 (USA) or 1-800-461-9120 (Canada). Gareth Stevens Publishing's Fax: (414) 225-0377.

Library of Congress Cataloging-in-Publication Data

20219

Schwartz, David M.
   Animal skin and scales / by David M. Schwartz; photographs by Dwight Kuhn.
      p. cm. — (Look once, look again)
   Includes bibliographical references and index.
   Summary: Introduces, in simple text and photographs, the outside coverings
of iguanas, butterflies, earthworms, snakes, fish, and turtles.
   ISBN 0-8368-2579-9 (lib. bdg.)
   1. Body covering (Anatomy)—Juvenile literature. 2. Skin—Juvenile literature.
[1. Ear. 2. Hearing. 3. Senses and sensation. 4. Animals—Physiology.] I. Kuhn,
Dwight, ill. II. Title. III. Series: Schwartz, David M. Look once, look again.
QL941.S38   2000
573.5—dc21   99-047589

This North American edition first published in 2000 by
Gareth Stevens Publishing
1555 North RiverCenter Drive, Suite 201
Milwaukee, Wisconsin 53212 USA

First published in the United States in 1998 by Creative Teaching Press, Inc., P. O. Box 6017, Cypress, California, 90630-0017.

Text © 1998 by David M. Schwartz; photographs © 1998 by Dwight Kuhn. Additional end matter © 2000 by Gareth Stevens, Inc.

Printed in the United States of America

1 2 3 4 5 6 7 8 9 04 03 02 01 00

ANIMAL SKIN & SCALES

by David M. Schwartz

photographs by Dwight Kuhn

Gareth Stevens Publishing
MILWAUKEE

These spines may remind you of a dinosaur, but this animal is alive today.

An iguana is not as tall as some dinosaurs, but it can reach almost 6 feet (2 meters) long. Its rough skin has hard, bumpy scales. A row of soft spines runs along its back and tail.

What insect's wings are covered with black and orange scales?

The scales on a monarch butterfly's wings overlap like shingles on a roof. The scales protect the wings. Under the scales, the wings are thin and clear.

This monarch has just come out of a case called a chrysalis. After its wings dry out, the butterfly will flutter away.

These short, stiff bristles help this animal move through the soil.

An earthworm's body is made of rings called segments. Each segment has bristles that grip the soil so the worm can move. The bristles also pick up vibrations in the soil to warn the worm of danger.

This skin is made of hard, colorful scales.

Snakes must shed the outer layer of their skin to get bigger, but they never shed their scales. Can you see the impression of the snake's scales on the old skin?

This brightly colored
fish is a famous fighter.

This male Siamese fighting fish is guarding its nest. When males see each other, they fight.

You won't have any trouble finding skin like this.

15

Just look at your fingertips! The ridges on them make a pattern called a fingerprint. No two people have exactly the same fingerprints. The ridges also help you feel and lift objects.

16

These are plates, but you wouldn't want to eat from them!

What animal has hard plates all over its back?

The box turtle wears a shell of hard plates that fit snugly together. It is a strong, protective dome.

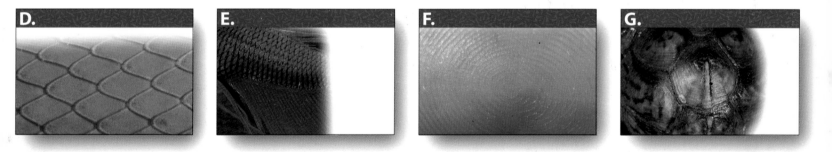

Look closely. To which animals do the skin or scales belong?

LOOK AGAIN

A. Iguana

B. Monarch butterfly

C. Earthworm

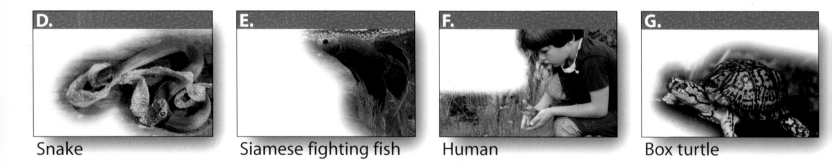

D. Snake

E. Siamese fighting fish

F. Human

G. Box turtle

How many were you able to identify correctly?

GLOSSARY

bristles: stiff, short, coarse hairs.

chrysalis: the pupa of a butterfly. The pupa is the stage in the life of an insect when it is changing from a larva into an adult.

dome: a natural formation that is shaped like a hemisphere. A hemisphere is half of a ball-shaped object.

iguana: a large lizard with a crest of small spines on its back that can be found from central Mexico to southern South America. Land iguanas feed on plants and animals. Marine iguanas feed on algae.

impressions: imprints that are formed and then left behind when an object has been under a certain amount of pressure from another object.

pattern: a design where shapes are repeated many times to form the whole.

plates: thin, flat, hard substances.

ridges: long, elevated parts of the body; long crests.

scales: small, flat, stiff plates that form the body covering of certain animals.

segments: sections or parts.

shed: to cast off a body covering.

spines: the sharp, pointed parts of the external body covering of certain animals.

vibrations: periodic motions that shake a solid object and make it quiver and tremble.

ACTIVITIES

Running Hot or Cold?

The iguana is a lizard, and lizards are cold-blooded. Their body temperature changes depending on the temperature of the air or water in the environment. Go to the library or search the Internet to see if you can discover which other animals are cold-blooded. Are people cold-blooded?

Endangered

Certain species of reptiles and amphibians are endangered. These include the leopard frog, the Mexican desert turtle, and the San Francisco garter snake, to name just a few. They are losing their habitat because of the increase in human development. Become involved in helping save endangered wildlife by contacting a nature organization in your area and asking how you can participate.

Saving the Day

Sometimes when it rains all day, water begins to collect on land. Because of the extra water on land, some turtles might wander away from their homes on the bank of a river or lake. When the land dries out again, the turtles might become stranded. If you see any wildlife in trouble like this, call your local humane society. They will be of help.

Only Skin Deep

Look at all the people around you, and look at the people on television and in the movies. As you know, people come in many different skin colors. Skin color comes from a pigment called melanin. Melanin also gives your hair and eyes their color. Do some research at the library and on the Internet to find out about this pigment that makes each of us our unique selves!

More Books to Read

Animal Survival (series). Michel Barré (Gareth Stevens)
Butterflies. The New Creepy Crawly Collection (series). Graham Coleman (Gareth Stevens)
Fangs! (series). Eric Ethan (Gareth Stevens)
Reptiles. Wonderful World of Animals (series). Beatrice MacLeod (Gareth Stevens)
Scaly Facts. Ivan Chermayefe (Harcourt)
Skin. Stephen Savage (Thomson Learning)
Why Do People Come in Different Colors? Isaac Asimov and Carrie Dierks (Gareth Stevens)

Videos

Armored Animals. (DK Publishing)
The Turtle Family. (Wood Knapp Video)
Worms and How They Live. (AIMS Multimedia)

Web Sites

onin.com/fp/fphistory.html
www.geocities.com/Rainforest/Vines/5504/index.html

Some web sites stay current longer than others. For further web sites, use your search engines to locate the following topics: *chrysalides, fingerprints, iguanas, scales, skin,* and *spines.*

INDEX